Praise for *Miracle*

Flora Wuellner has written a splendid book that not only makes the Gospel "stories of wonder" glow with light but also helps us invite wonder into our twenty-first-century souls. The social dimension of suffering, so often neglected in healing ministry, is woven into wise, gentle, and challenging meditations that speak directly to hearts that are wounded, lonely, afraid, despairing, or shamed. *Miracle* is a beautiful gift to all believers!

—TILDA NORBERG
United Methodist minister, Founder of Gestalt Pastoral Care,
Author of *Gathered Together: Creating Personal Liturgies for Healing and Transformation* and *Stretch Out Your Hand*

Anchored by decades of pastoral experience and deepened by the experience of personal loss, this book provides a straightforward and compassionate means by which the stories of Christ's miracles can enter anybody's life with power and honest comfort.

—BARBARA CAWTHORNE CRAFTON
Episcopal priest and author
Founder of the Geranium Farm (www.geraniumfarm.org),
Down-to-earth Support for Living

miracle

When
Christ
Touches
Our
Deepest
Need

FLORA SLOSSON WUELLNER

UPPER
ROOM BOOKS®
NASHVILLE

No part of this book may be reproduced in any manner whatsoever without written permission of the publisher except in brief quotations embodied in critical articles or reviews. For information, write Upper Room Books, 1908 Grand Avenue, Nashville, TN 37212.

The Upper Room® Web site: www.upperroom.org

UPPER ROOM®, UPPER ROOM BOOKS®, and design logos are trademarks owned by The Upper Room®, a ministry of GBOD®, Nashville, Tennessee. All rights reserved.

Unless otherwise noted, scripture quotations are from the New Revised Standard Version Bible, copyright 1989, Division of Christian Education of the National Council of the Churches of Christ in the United States of America. Used by permission. All rights reserved.

Scripture verses marked GNT are taken from the GOOD NEWS TRANSLATION, SECOND EDITION, Copyright © 1992 by American Bible Society. Used by permission. All rights reserved.

Cover design: Gore Studio, Inc. / www.gorestudio.com
Cover image: © Slawomir Jastrzebski / iStock
Interior design: Buckinghorse Design / www.buckinghorsedesign.com
First printing: 2008

Library of Congress Cataloging-in-Publication Data
Wuellner, Flora Slosson.
  Miracle : when Christ touches our deepest need / Flora Slosson Wuellner.
      p. cm.
  ISBN 978-0-8358-9963-5
  1. Jesus Christ—Miracles. 2. Spirituality. I. Title.
  BT366.3.W84 2008
  232.9'55—dc22   2008001786

Printed in the United States of America

To my husband, Wilhelm,
who opened to me the rich depths
of scripture for fifty years

contents

chapter 1

acts of wonder

He unrolled the scroll and found the place where it was
written:
    "The Spirit of the Lord is upon me,
        because he has anointed me
            to bring good news to the poor.
    He has sent me to proclaim
        release to the captives
      and recovery of sight to the blind,
        to let the oppressed go free,
    to proclaim the year of the Lord's favor."
. . . The eyes of all in the synagogue were fixed on him. Then
he began to say to them, "Today this scripture has been
fulfilled in your hearing."

                              —Luke 4:17-21

How did Jesus' face look when he first openly declared his
mission to heal, to release, to fulfill God's will and longing
to make us whole?

Perhaps we can picture his expression, the look in his eyes, as he laid hands on suffering people. We can sense his still intentness as he moved into the mystery and power of what we call a miracle, an act of wonder. We can imagine his eyes focused directly on the woman, man, or child who needed him. His eyes saw the pain below the pain, the hunger beneath the hunger, the face behind the face. We can sense the firm gentleness of his hands and the quiet clarity of his voice.

Surely Jesus felt the vast flood of God's merciful power flow through him as he looked at and touched the person who needed him. Divine healing poured not only into the body of the hurting person but also into that individual's deepest needs and pains: fear, shame, shock, loneliness. This power also poured into the community around each individual, and it flows to each of us two thousand years later. Miracles are still alive and active among us.

But in what way do miracles live and act among us? It seems clear that prayer helps increase immunity to disease, reduces anxiety and pain, and facilitates our response to medical treatment.

There is evidence that prayer often helps shorten convalescence; it certainly increases our alertness and peacefulness. But do miracles ever happen in the traditional sense in swift, complete, and medically unaccountable ways?

Fifty years ago, as a young pastor, I probably would have said no. But over the years I have become humbler, listening and observing more. Yes, acts of wonder still occur surprisingly often in this physical world.

I have personally known of cancers healed spontaneously after group prayer, an uncontrollable fibrillating heart returning to normal rhythm at the exact time a group prayed (at a distance), a sprained ankle healed instantly upon a group's touch, and a child's fall from a second-story window diverted from the concrete pavement directly below to a pile of leaves out of range as those watching prayed. These are only a few of the many unexplained occurrences I have witnessed.

The God we see through Jesus is always on the side of healing and wholeness.

However, such incidents raise more questions than they answer. All of us can think of accidents that weren't prevented, devastating illnesses that led to untimely death, hearts that failed even after prayer, and children who did hit the pavement.

Jesus never explained why suffering and disaster come so often to the good, the young, the innocent. But some things he made distinctly clear. He never believed or taught that God sends sickness and disaster as punishment or test. Only in very few healings did he refer to sin as connected with illness. His healings were not contingent on a person's piety or righteousness or a certain set of beliefs. Jesus healed all types of people—doubters, sinners, foreigners, persons of bad reputation.

The idea that an angry God sends disaster is a heresy handed down through the ages since pagan times. This is not the God we see revealed through Jesus. The God we see through Jesus always stands on the side of healing and wholeness. Even the cross to which Jesus invites us is not sickness or disaster. The cross is the burden of pain we freely lift from another to help carry and relieve.

If God does not send us illness or accidents, where do they come from? There are no simplistic answers. Partly they come from our own wrong choices, whether individual or communal. God gives us freedom to choose, and often our choices bring suffering to the innocent. But nature's storms, earthquakes, droughts and floods, lethal bacteria and viruses are not our choices. They are nature's imbalances and polarities, and nature is not God. Nature is one of God's creations that struggles in vast transitions.

A hundred years ago, my six-year-old uncle died agonizingly of scarlet fever. This child's illness was not caused by his sin or by the sins of his loving, religious family. God was neither punishing them nor making some moral point. Bacteria had attacked my uncle, and antibiotics had not yet been discovered; these miracle drugs were still embedded in the earth and in the minds of scientists yet to be born. One researcher described his work as "thinking God's thoughts after [God]." Our wisdom grows slowly, as does our love.

God's power, as best I can understand, is *self*-limited. I believe that rather than using force on us to bring about God's realm on earth, God wants us to grow in knowledge and wisdom. I believe God longs for us to delve into the mysteries of our planet, to discover the healing substances in nature's depths. I believe God wants us to learn to *care* enough to make medical research a high priority; to make our air, food, water, and soil healthy; to feed the hungry and bring treatment to the sick everywhere.

Learning to care—to feel compassion and responsibility—is the deep soul unfolding through which God's realm, God's will, becomes increasingly manifested on earth.

God does not stand apart from this transformation within and around us. It is a cosmic change, involving not only us humans but also nature itself. God works closely in, with, and through us as every atom, each cell, every thought and action open up to reveal God's love.

> For the creation waits with eager longing for the revealing of the children of God. . . . We know that the whole creation has been groaning in labor pains until now; and not only the creation, but we ourselves, who have the first fruits of the Spirit, groan inwardly while we wait for adoption, the redemption of our bodies.—Romans 8:19, 22-23

Sometimes, though, for reasons we do not completely understand, God's longing and power to heal pour through swiftly and fully, not waiting for the slow, groaning transformations of our choices or for the transitions of nature itself. Miracles of this type sometimes happen, but we can't predict their occurrence. We cannot put a miracle in a bottle and sell it. We do not know what blocks a full bodily miracle or what opens the door. We do know that God longs for everyone to be healed, because Jesus never refused to heal anyone, saying it was God's will that he or she remain sick.

Through Jesus, so closely united with God's own self, full healing was able to flow unimpeded. But as we reflect on his acts of wonder, we see that far more than bodily healing was involved. Each miracle has at least six levels of meaning, and each of these meanings directly affects us today. We may or may not (for reasons not fully understood) experience full bodily protection or cure, but the deeper meanings of the miracles will transform our lives.

Jesus' miracles show us that God's will, kingdom, or realm is characterized by compassion, mercy, limitless love.

1. *Through each of Jesus' acts of mercy we see God's nature.* We see what God wants, what God is like. Jesus' miracles show us that God's will, kingdom, or realm is characterized by compassion, mercy, limitless love. They show us that God's Spirit works actively among us like plants growing, like yeast working in bread dough. The work of the Spirit is not just something to hope for at the end of time.

2. *Jesus' miracles reveal God's passionate compassion for each individual.* Every person matters to God. No one gets lost in the crowd. Each one is unique, precious, beloved. Any form of religion or spirituality—any political or social theory that ignores, denies, or belittles the value of each individual—is destructive and dehumanizing and is not of God's Spirit.

3. *Jesus' miracles demonstrate God's longing for communal as well as individual healing.* These miracles show how Jesus tried to heal the spiritual sickness of villages, towns, families, religious organizations: their rigid mind-sets and ideologies, their exclusions, their lack of compassion, their fear and suspicion.

Communities are also wounded bodies; if unhealed, they can wound and imprison the minds and hearts of individual members for generations.

4. *Each of Jesus' acts of compassion helps us see that God cares about our earthly life.* Our earthly life matters. It is not a prison of the spirit or a low, unworthy, unspiritual condition. Our bodies, the world around us, our five senses are given to us as a sacrament, a unique way by which we become God's children, God's partners in this vast, divine cosmic adventure.

It is a difficult realm in which we live, this earthly life; it is similar to a birth process, as Paul described it. But we are destined for a glory beyond our imaginations. Therefore, each loving act we do through our bodily selves impacts the universe. We are all interconnected. To feed one another, clothe one another, help heal one another, and help lift one another's pain are divine acts within God's plan and love. Any religion or form of spirituality that proclaims that life in this material world is unimportant or degrading is a dehumanizing faith with terrible consequences.

> It is a difficult realm in which we live, this earthly life; it is similar to a birth process.
>
> ✎

5. *Jesus' miracles show us that God's healing and transformation involve the whole person:* heart, mind, spirit, body, relationships, and choices. God's loving power longs to enfold and flood through all that we are—our subconscious as well as conscious selves; our wounded memories; our damaged trust; our fears; our

shadow sides; our hidden hopes; the deep gifts within us not yet born or long forgotten; our attitudes toward ourselves, others, the world around us, and God. Perhaps the greatest act of wonder is that as we are healed, made whole, and filled with God, we become *more* our unique selves, not less. We are not identical products on a factory line; we are each individually handcrafted.

6. *The healing, transforming acts of Jesus have direct meaning and significance for each one of us in our daily lives.* They were not just events that happened two thousand years ago, trapped in history. Christ's ongoing, loving power is at work within and among us now, this day, this hour.

In this book I have chosen seven of Jesus' acts of wonder, each one showing a different need or hurt and the widely different ways those needs are expressed to God. In these stories we see the unique way Jesus responded to each need. In most of these stories we see all six levels of meaning with each miracle. I believe we each find ourselves in these stories.

As we read and reflect on each story, we can ask ourselves the following questions:

- What does this story tell me about what God is really like and how God feels about me?

- How does this story relate to my personal problems and questions right now?

- What meaning does it hold for what hurts me, and what I long for? How does it touch my deepest need?

- What does this story tell me about the communities in which I live—my family, my church, my workplace, my circle of friends?
- In what ways are my communities wounded? How does their woundedness affect me?
- How does this story change my feelings about myself, God, other people, or my life on this earth?
- As I reflect on this story, what new hopes or possibilities begin to open for me?

Let us move with the living Christ into God's acts of wonder.

chapter 2

the heart that hears us

As [Jesus] and his disciples and a large crowd were leaving
Jericho, Bartimaeus son of Timaeus, a blind beggar, was sitting by the roadside. When he heard that it was Jesus of
Nazareth, he began to shout out and say, "Jesus, Son of David,
have mercy on me!" Many sternly ordered him to be quiet, but
he cried out even more loudly, "Son of David, have mercy on
me!" Jesus stood still and said, "Call him here." And they
called the blind man, saying to him, "Take heart; get up, he is
calling you." So throwing off his cloak, he sprang up and came
to Jesus. Then Jesus said to him, "What do you want me to
do for you?"

—Mark 10:46-51

Years ago there was a musical drama called *Lost in the Stars*.
The title song wonders if God can hear our cries, our need,
in this vast universe with its billions of stars. Are we lost out
here among the stars with no one hearing or caring?

Each of us probably has wondered at some time if we are lost not only in the stars but also as individual persons among the millions of other people in this world. Do our own small needs matter among all these other countless needs?

When the doctor told me after my husband's exploratory surgery that Wilhelm's cancer, many years in remission, had returned and invaded his whole body, I realized he had only a few months to live. As he slept, I wandered off to the cafeteria for a cup of tea. I looked around at all the people coming and going, listened to the chatter around me and the clatter of trays and dishes, and wondered, *How can all this ordinary eating, drinking, talking, and daily work keep going on as if nothing drastic and life-changing has happened?* When we suffer traumatic loss or undergo radical change, it seems unbelievable that the sun rises and sets, traffic keeps rolling, and thousands go about their own business—even though our own sun stands still, and everything for us suddenly stops. Is there anyone who really hears or cares?

Bartimaeus, a blind beggar, sat on a busy street hoping for a handout. Had he sat in darkness all his life, or was his blindness a recent, shocking loss that also may have meant loss of job and total income? Scripture does not tell us. Whatever the case, he sat wrapped in his cloak, hearing people's chatter and the noise of footsteps all around him. Casual observers probably noticed him as a street fixture.

The Bible also does not say whether Bartimaeus had any family members or friends who helped him. Certainly he had no claim on the man he could hear approaching, Jesus from

Nazareth, whom many thought to be the Christ. But Bartimaeus was going to try his luck. From the excited talk around him, he gathered that this Jesus might pass right by him. Bartimaeus could not see him, of course, so he could not push his way through the crowd to get to him. Therefore he shouted to Jesus, loudly and persistently.

How foolish! How could Jesus possibly hear him, one lone voice among the crowd's uproar? How could Jesus even spot Bartimaeus in the crowd surrounding him? Even if by some miracle Jesus did hear him, why would he pause even for a moment as he walked the dangerous road to Jerusalem? There were so many needs. Jesus' mind would be on matters far more urgent than the needs of a blind beggar. Also, Jesus surely would be surrounded by his band of followers, who would guard their teacher from insignificant demands on his time and energy.

But Bartimaeus shouted for him anyway.

"Hush!" he was sternly told. Who did he think he was, shouting for the man who might be the Messiah, the one who had drawn the attention of the nation's wealthy and powerful?

Bartimaeus shouted even louder. What a strange, bold confidence in his call. Significantly he called Jesus "Son of David," one of the ancient terms for the yet-to-come anointed one who would bring healing and mercy to Israel.

"Jesus stood still," says verse 49. In itself this is an act of wonder. These words are among the most significant in scripture. "Jesus stood still." By this simple act we see directly into the heart of God, who not only hears each cry through the world's uproar but also *stands still*, turning full attention upon each of us as if we each were the only person in the universe.

Then another wondrous thing happened. "Call him here," said Jesus. He heard; he stood still; he then called forth. Bartimaeus must have felt already enfolded by miracle. Eagerly he jumped up, threw aside his cloak (perhaps his only possession?), and made his way to Jesus. Did someone guide his steps, perhaps the same person who had told him to keep still?

"What do you want me to do for you?" Jesus asked. What a strange question! Wasn't it obvious what Bartimaeus needed and wanted? What could matter more to him than his eyesight?

God's nature is to make us whole, and this work of renewal is active already among us.

Perhaps part of his healing was to openly express his need. Perhaps it was important that the crowd around him hear it. Perhaps an even deeper need, a deeper longing, would be touched.

This story shows us the depth of meanings in Jesus' miracles: the individual is precious to God; human need matters; the communal body also needs healing and loving renewal; God's nature is to make us whole, and this work of renewal is active already among us; and transformation involves our whole selves, not just the body. Not only was Bartimaeus's eyesight restored, but scripture also tells us that after this healing, he became one of Jesus' followers. No longer disregarded and purposeless, Bartimaeus became a person who could give, follow a new light, love within a new fellowship.

This story reaches through two thousand years with power and significance. What does it mean for each of us?

I remember wondering as a child during my bedtime prayer, *What if only* once *in my life I was allowed to speak directly to* God *and be heard?* It was a startling, almost scary, thought. This act of prayer that I rattled off (when I remembered) at bedtime—what did it really mean? What was happening? As I asked myself this question, though I did not hear an outer voice, a response seemed to rise deep within me, full of loving laughter: "There's a lot more to it all than you realize!" I was about nine years old, and I think this may have been my first consciously aware contact with God.

If only once in our lifetime we were permitted to pray to the Creator of the universe and know we were heard, it would be the supreme moment of our lives. How we would think about it, prepare for it years ahead. How excitedly we would share our experience with others. How we would remember it for the rest of our lives with awed gratitude, that awesome time when we received God's full attention. Nothing else could compare.

Bartimaeus's story reveals the miracle that God's heart gives us full attention at any moment we choose—and calls us closer. This is what prayer is.

For some of us, if we had this gift only once in a lifetime, it would perhaps be enough just to be in God's presence, open to the glory of that gaze, breathing in that breath of life. This is one of the most healing, transforming ways to pray. For some, it is all they ever need.

But as we see in this story, God invites us to speak, to express our needs and longings. Jesus never told anyone that his or her needs were trivial or not spiritual enough. He told no one, "Get your mind on higher things!" Surprisingly often the surface need is fulfilled, but because God longs to heal our whole selves, we can expect surprising new doors to open and unexpected new ways of life to be offered.

"Each faculty tasked / To perceive Him has gained an abyss, where a dewdrop was asked," I read in a poem many years ago.[1]

"I'm lonely; I want more friends. I never have any fun. But I'm too shy to go new places and reach out to people. Is that a stupid thing to ask God about?" a young woman once asked me.

"Nothing is too stupid to ask God about," I told her. "God cares about your loneliness. It matters. Pray about it, and be ready for surprises."

The young woman did pray about her desire to gain new friends. No overnight changes occurred, but during the next few weeks, unexpected doors began to open: a couple of acquaintances invited her to join them in a project. Shyly she agreed and began to meet new people in a nonthreatening way. As her confidence grew, she began at first timidly, then with more confidence, to reach out to others. She started to discover surprising gifts of organization and leadership within herself. Her deeper, richer self began to unfold. Today she works with troubled children and teenagers from dysfunctional families, often speaking to large groups. She loves the work, and it feels natural to her.

God listens to our surface longings with compassion and then reaches to the deeper needs and gifts buried within us.

Each of us has an inner Bartimaeus crying out, often unheard or ignored by those around us and sometimes even by ourselves. My ministry radically changed when I realized that what we call our negative sides—anger, anxiety, complaining, criticizing, procrastinating, controlling, and so on—are usually deep inner cries for help. Perhaps they are cries from early childhood, rising from emotional wounds that never healed. We were told so often to get over them, rise above them, forgive and forget, concentrate on the positive, that we thrust down these unhealed wounds below our conscious level.

But wounds do not just go away. If unhealed, they cry like abandoned children in the dark, forgotten places within us. The only way they can make their presence felt is through our negative attitudes, our addictive escapes, all symptoms of pain.

Some forms of spiritual therapy attend only to the symptoms and ignore the underlying suffering. Too often we are told that feelings like anger, fear, doubt, or persistent grief show lack of faith in God, or that Satan causes them. In recent years an unhealthy emphasis on Satan has surfaced in Christian circles. Jesus, though obviously aware of the existence of evil, only rarely mentions Satan. His main emphasis was healing the deep pain of the world.

Once I participated in a church camp ritual in which we were told to write our worst faults, our most negative attitudes, on a piece of paper and then cast the paper into a bonfire as we paraded past, singing a hymn. These actions were supposed to symbolize the destruction of our faults, but of course those same faults rose again vigorously within twenty-four hours. They were not destroyed because they were the inner cries that God wanted us to listen to and bring to God's hands for healing.

"What do you want me to do for you?" Jesus asked Bartimaeus, and God asks us the same question now. It is so important that we name our hurt, saying it to God, who knows about it already, because we need to listen to ourselves saying it.

Then we need to look with God at the even deeper wounds and name them also. God works through trusted friends or therapists to help us explore our deepest hurts. Whatever we discover, whatever we name that lies within us, will not shock or alienate God, who already knows all about it.

Will physical healing also occur as the inner cries are heard and healed? Often it does happen, because so frequently bodily illnesses are intertwined with unhealed emotional hurts. If someone's body cannot be completely cured, the person may experience a release from pain or respond more swiftly to medical treatment. Certainly anxiety, stress, and tension can be healed even if the physical body cannot be cured. New ways of loving and relating to others, as well as richer, deeper insight and creativity, will open to us.

After my husband, Wilhelm, was first diagnosed with cancer, he lived many more years with a far deeper quality of life. He was not physically cured, but with the help of alternative and standard medicine, he lived well and vigorously. During those years his spiritual life deepened, and his ability to respond to others became even warmer and more intuitive. He learned to listen to himself, to his childhood suffering and fear during the Nazi years in Germany, to his terror of war and air raids. With eager joy he learned how to meditate and reduce everyday stress, and he discovered new, holistic ways of eating and exercising. He began to paint pictures, something he had always longed to do but had never made time for in his busy life as pastor and teacher. He researched his illness in depth and counseled many other men diagnosed with the same cancer. He believed his later years to be the most vital and richest ones of his life.

When his condition became terminal and the time approached to leave his body with the loving help of hospice care, Wilhelm grieved over leaving us, but he knew with certainty that beautiful new adventures lay ahead.

"Grandfather, how does it feel to die?" our eleven-year-old granddaughter asked him with deep, straightforward concern. He looked thoughtful and then replied, "It is a mixture of sorrow and joy, as with any great change." As his bodily weakness increased, I often heard him whispering to God as he released himself into the Hands of mercy.

> What no eye has seen, nor ear heard,
>   nor the human heart conceived,
> what God has prepared for those who love him.
> —1 Corinthians 2:9

I was like Bartimaeus during those months when I was caregiver for my husband. I learned all over again that God hears the cries of the heart. We are not lost in the stars; we are seen and heard. God stands still and calls us forth. God's love flowed to me through the tenderness of family and friends. God gave me incredible dreams in which tall angels of light and comfort filled our house. My grief, my irrational flashes of anger at my husband leaving me, the "why me, why us?" self-pitying moods, and my anxiety over the future responsibilities facing me as a widow were all understood and embraced. I learned not to feel shame over these negative moods but to name them honestly to God, knowing they rose from natural human fatigue and sorrow.

I felt guided gently but firmly to care for myself as well for my husband. The inner certainty grew that he and I would not be cut off from each other when his body died, but that we would continue growing together in our partnership of love and spiritual adventure.

"What do you want me to do for you?" God asks and then opens doors we never dreamed of.

Notes on the Reflections and Meditations in This Book

All of the reflections and meditations are voluntary. If any meditation is unhelpful, painful, or makes you anxious, move into another form of prayer, or leave the meditation altogether. You can always return to any meditation later if you choose. Move very slowly through each meditation, feeling free to change any symbols or imagery for yourself.

If you guide others through a meditation, make clear that it is a voluntary process, and each participant is free to leave the meditation or to change the symbolic imagery.

If any meditation causes deep pain or anxiety, talk about those feelings with a trusted friend or therapist.

Reflection and Meditation

Jesus stood still and said, . . .
"What do you want me to do for you?"

—Mark 10:49, 51

Make your body comfortable, whether sitting, lying down, or standing. Take a few slow, deep breaths; then breathe naturally.

You are not alone. God's tenderness surrounds you. Rest in God's deep strength. You are in a safe place.

You may feel nothing special. Do not force any feelings. Just remind yourself that God's attention enfolds you. God hears and knows your deepest needs, your inner hurts, your deepest longings. Gently breathe in this presence. This may be all you need at this time, just resting and breathing in God's love.

But if you feel ready, think of some special deep need. God already knows about it, but express it anyway. Be as plain and direct as possible. Name the need. Then take a few quiet moments to rest in God's love. This may be as far as you wish to go at this time.

If you feel ready, talk to God about some inner fault or stumbling block that makes life harder for yourself and others.

Perhaps constant anxiety, ongoing anger, overcontrol, jealousy, fear of intimacy, some addictive habit, or another characteristic or behavior spoils your inner peace.

Do you think this inner, ongoing problem may have risen from some early hurt or abuse of trust? Perhaps you do not know where it comes from. Think of or picture God lifting this inner "problem child," holding it, listening to it, and laying hands of healing on it. Resting your body in this safe presence, breathe gently and slowly as God enfolds your inner problem with healing, transforming light. Do you sense anything changing within you? Take all the time you need. You can return to this inner healing as often as you wish.

When you feel ready, stretch a bit, gently massage your face and hands, and quietly leave your meditation, knowing that God's healing love still enfolds you.

---

1. From "Saul" by Robert Browning (1812–1889).

chapter 3

the voice that calms and carries us

On that day, when evening had come, [Jesus] said to them, "Let us go across to the other side." And leaving the crowd behind, they took him with them in the boat, just as he was. . . . A great windstorm arose, and the waves beat into the boat, so that the boat was already being swamped. But he was in the stern, asleep on the cushion; and they woke him up and said to him, "Teacher, do you not care that we are perishing?" He woke up and rebuked the wind, and said to the sea, "Peace! Be still!" Then the wind ceased, and there was a dead calm.

—Mark 4:35-39

Sometimes we do not call out in bold faith like Bartimaeus; we scream (at least inwardly) in panic. When threatening, out-of-control events roar around us and the world rocks under our feet, we cry out in fear and outrage: "God, my life is going to pieces! Don't you care? Are you *sleeping*?"

One of my dear friends stood in her living room, dizzy with flu and fever, fists clenched, desperate. Her marriage was collapsing. She hated her job but knew her three young children depended on her salary. Every road seemed blocked. Coughing and sick with despair, she felt she could hardly breathe. Maybe she would die right there in her living room.

Inwardly she screamed to God. Then something happened. "Light surrounded me and held me firmly," she told me. "I felt taken to another place. A voice said, 'When I guide you to a different life, it will not be through the path of illness and despair but through peace and an open door.'"

The voice ceased; the light vanished. She was back in her living room breathing normally, her flu symptoms gone. Within a few months another job opportunity opened for her; she loved her new work and served in that position for many years. The awe, strength, and peace have never left her heart since then.

"Tell me again about the voice," I asked.

"It was strong, direct, and firm, not a soothing pat on the head," she answered. "Compassionate, yes, but full of authority. I had felt like the ground was tossing and swirling below me, but when the voice spoke, I felt as if I were totally safe on the strongest rock in the universe."

My husband and I once almost bought a beautiful wood carving of Jesus standing in the boat, calming the storm. We had never before seen a carving of that story. What held us back was the expression on Jesus' face as he commanded the wind and waves. It was not a face of stern, empowered love. He simply looked cross. No wave or wind would have bothered to obey the irritable expression of one merely annoyed at being wakened from a nap.

Several years ago my husband fell off a six-foot ladder onto concrete pavement. When I reached him, he was only semiconscious. Outwardly I was a model of cool efficiency. I knew not to move him; I knew to send for an ambulance; I knew to cover him and speak to him calmly. Inside I was a shocked, churning mess! In the emergency room the attendants tried to stop me from going to my husband, who was asking for me. By the time the physician arrived, I was shaking from head to foot with shock and anger.

The doctor sized up my condition at a glance; took my cold, shaking hands in hers; and said in a voice of calm, firm authority, "Of course you can sit with your husband. I will take you to him. But you're in shock. Stand still and take a few slow, deep breaths. That's right; breathe very slowly and deeply. You're doing fine." Warmth flooded me, and I stopped shaking. We smiled at each other, and she led me to my husband.

I believe that Jesus spoke with such a voice both to the panicked disciples and to the storm—not with irritable, scolding, or angry shouts but not merely soothing either. The word *rebuke* means a sharp, clear correction. When we are gripped by panic, it is calm, firm authority that reaches us best through the turbulence around us and our pounding hearts within us.

Most of us will not see light or hear the divine voice like my friend did in her living room. But the empowered Healer is as fully with us in our tossing boats as he was in that boat on the Sea of Galilee. Christ stands in risen power with us, just as that physician stood with me in the emergency room—holding our hands, breathing with us, calming our hearts.

When fear begins to overwhelm us, we can think of the living Christ, whose heart and voice are God's heart and voice, speaking to us inwardly:

> I am here. I will not leave you. Hold onto me. You are safe with me. Breathe slowly. Breathe deeply. My healing breath of life is flowing into you. Take my peace into your body. Take my peace into your heart.

Biblical historians tell us that early Christians paid close attention to this story of Jesus stilling the storm and took great comfort from it. For them the boat symbolized the church, beset with the storms of persecution and the storms of its own communal disagreements. They reminded one another that though the Christ seemed to be sleeping, in actuality he was awake at depth, watching over them and guiding them through any storm that threatened them.

I have never forgotten one spiritual group that brought a stopwatch to all its business and planning meetings. Every half hour the one whose turn it was to hold the watch called a break of five minutes for shared silence. Miraculously, no matter what disagreements had arisen in the discussion, a calmer, clearer atmosphere always followed the silence. Such a communal turning to the inner, shared pool of quiet goes far beyond a mere time-out or cooling-off period. When a church or family group uses the quiet space for slow, deep breathing and a recognition of the sovereign Love among them, a different emotional and spiritual dimension prevails when the discussion resumes.

Storms, though they can be destructive, are not a moral evil. Nature's storms are a balancing of electrical polarities and charges, just as earthquakes are nature's way of equalizing the built-up pressures of the moving continental plates beneath us. Likewise, the emotional storms within us are not in themselves evil. They arise when strain and stress throw our emotional energies out of balance. But as with nature's extremes, when anger and fear spin out of control, they lead to devastation. Anger is a huge power, like a strong wind or a gigantic wave. Recently it occurred to me that God does not destroy great energies but can balance them, using that power for a creative purpose. When we feel an out-of-control anger arising within us—for example, when a speeding car tailgates us or passes us on a dangerous curve—we can ask God to take the power of the anger into God's own heart, cleanse it of toxicity, and use it in another way. Otherwise we either try to suppress the anger, which then eats into our body and our inner peace, or we allow it to explode into dangerous retaliation.

The storm of fears within us also holds vast power. It is called the fight-or-flight response. In prehistoric times, such emotional power was necessary for human survival. But fear, like anger, when out of control, can tear us apart. This power too, when it arises in us as panic, can be given to God's heart and hands. No long meditations or wordy prayers are necessary. We can say a prayer of swift release:

God, take the great power of this anger (or fear) out of my body and heart. Put it into your own heart to use for good.

The swift, immense change and release within us is a miracle that never ceases to awe me.

I believe we are on a great frontier of learning how to pray for the vast *communal* storms of this world—the storms of ancient hatreds, anger, fear that rage among nations, races, ethnic groups, religions. What radical healings would unfold if our religious communities did not just vaguely pray for peace, but specifically offered up these communal tempests to God's heart to heal and cleanse them of their toxic power?

Not only did Jesus calm the raging storm on the lake and soothe the panic of his friends, but also he implanted a vibrant peace in their hearts, a cleansed and creative energy. The New Revised Standard Version speaks of a "dead calm" that followed the storm. I prefer the wording in older translations such as the King James Version: "a great calm." There is nothing whatever dead about the shalom, the living peace, Christ gives us. It is alert, alive, and strong beyond description.

The disciples would need that special peace when they landed on the other side of the lake. They found themselves among the Gerasenes, in an uneasy, conflicted country of mixed races and religions. There they were confronted by a violent demoniac whose community feared and rejected them even after Jesus healed him. Difficult hours and hard work lay ahead of them, but the great energy of inner peace that had replaced the inner storm of fear remained within them. In the same way, my friend who experienced the light and the voice that healed her panic still had hard work and decisions ahead of her. But vibrant peace remains the center of her life.

As the power of peace enfolds us, we too ask, as the disciples asked, "Who then is this, that even the wind and the sea obey him?" (v. 41).

Reflection and Meditation

> He . . . rebuked the wind, and said to the sea, "Peace! Be still!"—Mark 4:39

Relax your body in whatever way works best for you. Take a few deep, slow breaths; then breathe naturally.

You are held safely within God's strong and gentle presence. You can rest your full bodily weight upon that presence. Rest quietly, breathing in that presence even if you feel nothing special. This may be all you need at this time.

But if you feel ready, think of a time in your life when you felt a storm around or within you. Was it caused by a sudden shock? an accident or illness? a loss of job? a betrayal of trust? a family upheaval? a threatened loss? Do not try to live through it emotionally now; just bring it to memory and look at it from a safe distance. Did anything or anyone help you then? What or who helped?

Does this memory still cause anxiety, anger, or other discomfort within you? Picture or think of Jesus standing next to you during that experience, enfolding you with a sense of strength and comfort. Hear Jesus saying to the out-of-control events: "Be quiet. Calm down. Peace!"

Imagine Jesus turning to you and saying: "That storm is healed now. It has no power over you. You are healed from the fear (or anger or shock) it caused you."

Quietly rest, knowing that the impact of that memory is held and healed in God's heart.

This may be all you need right now. But if you feel ready, ask yourself, *Is there a storm around or within me right now? Or may a storm threaten to come?* Picture or think of Jesus standing with you, holding you with strength, smiling at you, and saying: "I am here. I won't leave you. I am calming the storm. I am calming your heart. You are wrapped in my warmth and peace. I am guiding each of your steps. Breathe in my presence. Breathe in my strength. Breathe in my peace."

Think of or picture the storm's power—whether fear, anger, shock—flowing into God's heart, out of your body like a great wind or wave moving away from you.

Is somebody you know and care about experiencing a life storm? Think of or picture the strong Christ near that person, wrapping him or her in a cloak of light and peace, breathing on that person the slow, deep breath of peace.

When you feel ready, gently stretch, lightly massage your face and hands, and move quietly out of your meditation.

chapter 4

the strength that empowers us

Now there was a woman who had been suffering from hemorrhages for twelve years. She had endured much . . . and had spent all that she had; and she was no better, but rather grew worse. She had heard about Jesus, and came up behind him in the crowd and touched his cloak. . . . Immediately her hemorrhage stopped. . . . Immediately aware that power had gone forth from him, Jesus turned about in the crowd and said, "Who touched my clothes?" . . . He looked all around to see who had done it. But the woman, knowing what had happened to her, came in fear and trembling, fell down before him, and told him the whole truth. He said to her, "Daughter, your faith has made you well; go in peace, and be healed of your disease."

—Mark 5:25-27, 29-30, 32-34

Bartimaeus had boldly called out his need. The disciples had screamed out their fear and anger at the top of their voices.

But this woman (we never know her name) moved toward Jesus silently, secretively, and in shame.

She had reason for her silence. As a bleeding person, she was considered by the orthodox to be unclean, contaminated, untouchable. For twelve years she had not been embraced or touched, even by her family. She could not nurse them when they were sick or comfort them in her arms. As she walked down the street, people carefully moved aside lest they touch her.

Scripture tells us she had spent all her money for cures but was getting worse. Deeper than the exhaustion of her chronic illness and the loss of her resources, though, must have been her loneliness and sense of shame. It is hard not to internalize what others think of us. She probably thought of herself as unworthy and unclean. How could she possibly believe that Jesus would deliberately touch her or encourage her to touch him?

Also, if others saw her touching him, they would consider him contaminated also, unfit to do God's work until he had been purified. Jesus was on his way to heal the dying daughter of Jairus, an important man in the community. If by her touch she prevented this, she would be blamed. She might be cast out of the community altogether.

Hers was a silent cry for a secret healing—a quick, shamed touch on his outer garment. She hoped no one would notice, especially not Jesus. Maybe the help would come through in a private, solitary way.

When I read this story, I think of so many people who are exhausted, drained, overwhelmed, and desperate for help but who cannot cry their need aloud, do not want others to know how they feel. Many men and women in the helping professions—pastors, social workers, counselors, therapists, medical workers—are chronically exhausted, their energies drained away. They dare not admit to themselves, let alone others, that they have reached their limits.

"You must be exhausted," I said to a surgeon I was consulting as he rushed into the examining room. I knew he had just come from a major operation. His waiting room was full of patients yet to be seen. Dark circles were around his eyes, and he looked very pale.

"Not at all, not at all," he replied hurriedly and defensively. But just a few months later he gave up his practice and resigned.

I think also of those caregivers at home who never take breaks, and of those who feel overwhelmed with family responsibilities or constantly fill in for others at their workplace. A dear friend was due at a family reunion. As the time drew near, she developed mysterious bodily pains. She began to wake at night, reviewing memories of old, unhealed generational family wounds. She was the "strong" one of the family, the one everyone looked to, expecting her to make peace and hold it all together. She phoned me, almost weeping in conflict and guilt. How could she possibly tell them she was too tired to come? They all depended on her. How could she be so weak as to let them down? Surely it was God's will that she go, even if those gatherings hurt and exhausted her. How ashamed she felt!

I think also of those who have experienced abuse from their

family or friends. We often wonder why abuse victims stay in the abusive situation, quietly enduring it. Why don't they leave? Why don't they speak up, protest, call for help? There are many reasons.

One major reason is shame. Abuse victims are ashamed that one they have loved or cared for is capable of hurting them. This horrible fact is too appallingly embarrassing to make public.

> **Abuse victims are ashamed that one they have loved or cared for is capable of hurting them.**
>
> ☙

Sometimes they feel personal shame—perhaps they deserved the punishment; perhaps after all they are bad persons, unworthy of better treatment. They may feel so unworthy that they believe they cannot possibly live a successful life away from the abuser. Others may mistreat them also. Eventually they become so tired and drained that submitting to what is familiar is easier than moving into a new, possibly threatening, way of life. These too are the silent sufferers, the secret touchers.

But Jesus instantly felt the woman's secret, desperate touch even among the jostling crowd around him. *Why did he make it public?* He must have known she was ashamed and frightened. Wouldn't it have been more compassionate for him to let it remain a silent exchange of need and healing? Why put this woman, already so humiliated, through the public ordeal of speaking before them all?

Only recently did I understand the implications. Jesus knew that not only had the woman been a victim of exhausting, draining illness, but also her community had treated her mercilessly through their rejection and exclusion. She needed more than bodily healing. She needed to speak aloud the truth of her hurt, loneliness, despair, and shame. She needed to hear herself telling the whole truth before them all.

She needed also to hear Jesus tell her openly, in front of everyone, that she was a worthy, faithful person. He called her "daughter." Only in this particular story (also recorded in Matthew and Luke) does Jesus refer to a woman as his daughter. How deeply she must have needed that word of intimacy and respect. With his tenderness and peace (shalom), Jesus gave her not only bodily healing but also the deeper healing of her heart and spirit.

Her entire community needed to hear the whole truth also. Her community was sicker than she was, with the spiritual disease of merciless, rigid exclusion of others. The community needed healing, and communal healing is much more difficult than individual healing.

The community members needed to see and to hear that God's love excludes no one. They needed to learn that compassionate mercy matters far more than rules. They needed to hear her share the pain she had undergone; they needed to see how Jesus honored her faith, and that he was not rendered unclean by her touch. They needed Jesus' witness that it is not God's will for anyone to remain sick, drained, lonely, uncomforted. As Jesus challenged the ancient, cruel laws, he was revealing to them what God's kingdom really is.

I believe also that Jesus made this story public because he wanted us to hear it through the centuries, beyond that time and place, to touch each of us today. I believe he wants each of us now to hear what God says to our hearts when we are exhausted, drained, ashamed, or abused:

> You are my beloved child. As you stretch your hands of silent need to me, I feel your touch in my heart. I honor your need. My love and strength flow out to you. Let me heal your shame. Let me help you to speak your need openly to others as well as to me, so that others may also be healed by hearing the whole truth.

The healing of our inner wounds of abuse or the healing of our exhaustion from limitless caregiving cannot remain a private matter between ourselves and God. It must become a communal matter. Those around us need to know for their sake as well as our own that caregivers also need care, that shepherds of others are also sheep who need feeding, that limits and boundaries must be honored, that sabbaths of the spirit and body are not selfish indulgences but commanded by God. If we have been exhausted and diminished by abuse, the whole community needs to hear it openly stated that God does not tolerate abuse of any kind, whether physical, emotional, verbal, or spiritual.

In his powerful chapter on God as the good shepherd, Ezekiel speaks prophetic words he hears from God:

> Therefore, thus says the Lord GOD to them: I myself will judge between the fat sheep and the lean sheep. Because you pushed with flank and shoulder, and butted at all the weak

animals with your horns . . . , I will save my flock, and they shall no longer be ravaged; and I will judge between sheep and sheep. —Ezekiel 34:20-22

Abuse and tyranny have no part in God's sovereign realm. Exclusion has no place in God's heart. When we are victimized, God asks us to tell "the whole truth" openly, to set limits without shame, so that all may be healed.

I talked with a middle-aged man who for years had been a faithful member of a church fellowship. This church had dominated his personal life, regularly exposing him to communal shame when he had doubts, made mistakes, or asked questions. They laid upon him, as well as on other members, burdens of guilt and anxiety. He endured this life in sick silence, believing it was God's will for him. Surely, he felt, he must be unworthy, must somehow deserve these communal reproaches. As time went on, he began to have deep, restless doubts. He visited other churches, observed other ways of living the Christian life. When he finally left the fellowship, he kept silent about those years of communal abuse.

Together we shared the story of the bleeding woman, healed by Jesus not only of her bodily illness and exhaustion but also healed of her many years of silent shame during the communal rejection. With the help of this story, he began to share openly his own whole truth with others. Today he helps other victims out of their abusive prisons.

For many years I kept a length of plain blue cotton cloth to hold during my prayer time. I had received the cloth at a retreat that was centered around the story of the bleeding woman. "Think of this cloth as Jesus' garment," the worship leader suggested. "Respond to it in whatever way you need to. You can hold it in your hands or wrap it around your hands. You might hold it to your face or wrap it around your head or shoulders. Then tell Jesus the whole truth of your need, your hurt, your shame."

Eventually I shared the story and gave the cloth to someone who deeply needed it. But I still remember how I felt when I touched it. During times of fatigue, shame, and loneliness I inwardly touch Jesus' garment and feel new strength flowing into me. But I try also to remember the whole story, that exhaustion and draining cannot be kept as a private matter between myself and God. I must share what I feel with others who are involved and work together to find ways by which limits are set, boundaries maintained, and times of rest and renewal are claimed.

If any form of abuse has been involved—any attempt to humiliate, diminish, dominate, manipulate, or exclude, this story reminds me that this behavior too cannot be kept a secret between myself and God. For the sake of others as well as myself, I need to tell the whole truth openly in Christ's presence for the empowered release of us all.

A beloved passage from Paul's letter to the church in Ephesus is a powerful guide:

> But speaking the truth in love, we must grow up in every way into him who is the head, into Christ, from whom the whole body, joined and knit together . . . , promotes the body's growth in building itself up in love. —Ephesians 4:15-16

Reflection and Meditation

She . . . came up behind him in the crowd and touched his cloak.—Mark 5:27

Rest your body comfortably. Take a few slow, deep breaths and then breathe naturally.

You are in a safe place, within God's love. With each gentle breath you take, breathe in God's breath of life.

When you feel ready, ask yourself if you are feeling chronically tired, drained, pushed to the limit.

Do many people depend on you? Do you feel ashamed if you set limits? Do you usually feel you should be doing more, that you are not fulfilling your ideals for yourself? Do you feel unworthy and embarrassed if you need help from others?

Do you feel ashamed of yourself as a person? Do you feel this shame or sense of unworthiness arises from some childhood or adolescent experience? Or has it resulted from some recent abuse or exclusion? Did something happen that made you feel unworthy of being loved for yourself?

It is hard to look at these feelings, even when held in God's love. Take your time and move slowly through these thoughts, and remember you are in a safe place with God.

If it helps you, think about holding Jesus' cloak in your hands or wrapping it about your head and shoulders. (You may wish to use a real cloth.) Love and strength are flowing into you.

When you feel ready, try to tell the Healer exactly what you feel. Tell the Healer if you have felt pushed, overworked, drained, controlled by others. Tell the Healer if you feel you have been abused or excluded in a way that made you feel unworthy. Be as honest and direct as possible.

Relax your body, and become aware of your slow, steady breathing. You are safe.

Still holding on to the Healer, ask God to show you ways to be open and honest with others about your needs. Ask God to show you ways to set limits.

Ask for healing of your exhaustion, your sense of unworthiness, your shame. Know that a way will unfold for you. Let God tell you that you are worthy and loved.

Rest, breathing gently and quietly. When you feel ready, stretch and lightly massage your face and hands, and leave the meditation quietly.

* * *

If this meditation has caused deep pain or anxiety, discuss your situation with someone you trust as soon as possible. God works powerfully not only through prayer but also through other people who care and are trained to hear and help.

chapter 5

the hand that holds and guides us

Immediately he made the disciples get into the boat and go on ahead to the other side. . . . he went up the mountain by himself to pray. When evening came he was there alone, but by this time the boat, battered by the waves, was far from the land, for the wind was against them. And early in the morning he came walking toward them on the sea. But when the disciples saw him walking on the sea, they were terrified, saying, "It is a ghost!" And they cried out in fear. But immediately Jesus spoke to them and said, "Take heart, it is I; do not be afraid."

Peter answered him, "Lord, if it is you, command me to come to you on the water." He said, "Come." So Peter got out of the boat, started walking on the water, and came toward Jesus. But when he noticed the strong wind, he became frightened, and beginning to sink, he cried out, "Lord, save me!" Jesus immediately reached out his hand and caught him, saying to him, "You of little faith, why did you doubt?" When they got into the boat, the wind ceased.

—Matthew 14:22-32

This is another storm story, but it differs from the earlier one, speaking to different needs. This storm was not a deadly one. The disciples were working hard in heavy turbulence with high wind and waves, but the boat was not sinking. They probably wondered why everything was so difficult when they were simply trying to obey Jesus' request to take the boat to the other side of the lake while he took some deeply needed time alone to pray.

Lately, things had been generally hard for them. On their recent visit to Jesus' hometown, Nazareth, the people there took offense at Jesus' teaching and rejected them.

Then came the horrifying news of the execution of John the Baptist, Jesus' cousin and their friend. Added to that shock and grief was the fact that the ruling powers were hostile toward them and were watching Jesus closely.

And now, after the intensity of caring for and feeding the crowds that followed Jesus, the disciples had to cope with this exhausting, stormy row across the lake. Where was Jesus anyway? Shouldn't he have stayed near them when they were having such a tough time and only were trying to do what he asked?

Then, out of the dark, appeared a human form walking toward them on the water. This was too much! Was it a ghost, a sure sign of impending death? Or perhaps it was one of those evil spirits Jesus had been casting out, coming in revenge!

A beloved voice rang out across the water, strong and hearty. But was it really Jesus? The disciples were filled with doubt. So Peter challenges the voice and the apparition. Some translations record Peter as saying, "Lord, if it is really you . . ." He puts the person on the water to the test. If it actually is Jesus, he will obey the test and give Peter the power to walk on the water toward him.

To me, this is the crux of the story. Only recently did this storm story reveal another possible meaning from what I had always been taught. We have usually been told that Peter's effort to walk on water was a noble act of well-meaning faith, and his sudden fear and failure of his faith were what caused him to sink. Suddenly for me, the whole picture changed, and I saw myself in a new and unexpected light. It was not Jesus' plan or guidance that Peter leave the boat and walk on water. Jesus had asked only one thing: that the disciples take the boat across the lake to the other side. When he came to them in the battering wind and called out to them in reassurance, he did *not* tell them to prove their faith by leaving the boat. On the contrary, he was coming to *them*, moving swiftly across the waves.

It was Peter's bright idea to leave the boat. Peter was notorious for his sudden bright ideas. Exactly why did he want to do this? First, he was challenging Jesus to prove that it was really he. Peter may also have wanted to prove his own faith and courage—especially after that shameful display of fear. Perhaps he wanted to be able to do all the things Jesus did. Perhaps he acted on the impulse of his warm, reckless love. Probably it was a combination of all these motives.

I asked myself, is it possible that Peter was acting *outside* God's guidance? Was his urge to walk on water a temptation, just as Jesus had been tempted earlier to throw himself off the pinnacle of the temple to prove God's favor and power? (Matt. 4:5-7).

After all, Peter was abandoning ship, leaving the others to the task of rowing the boat in heavy weather.

How often had I told God what to do, rather than asked what God wanted me to do?

I asked myself the uncomfortable question, how often had I left *my* boat, taken risks and chances that God had not asked of me? How often had I tried to test God's presence, favor, or power by leaping out of my given task to stride on water when God had asked me only to take my boat across to the other side? How often had I told God what to do, rather than asked what God wanted me to do?

I remembered the times when I had volunteered for extra responsibilities and tasks that I knew (if I were being honest) were beyond my real strength and energy and threatened my major priorities. *God will keep me going,* I assumed, proud of my faith, as I threw myself into some righteous cause or fascinating project. If I bothered to pray about a decision, it was usually (as with Peter) to tell God to give permission and strength. After all, if the project was worthy, then of course God would want me to do it. No asking necessary. How easily I forgot the warning a spiritual leader gave me when I graduated from seminary: "Watch that you do not go faster than God's grace."

How often did I begin to sink like Peter? Every time! There are so many signs of sinking. We begin to feel overwhelmed, breathless, anxious, irritable. We begin to feel like misunderstood martyrs with no one, let alone God, taking note of all the wonderful things we are doing. Or if someone does notice and warn us, we impatiently bat this person aside as someone who has no faith. We find our undone daily tasks piling up. Perhaps we sleep poorly with restless dreams. Strange bodily symptoms appear. Inner peace has vanished. We feel out of control, or too controlling, or perhaps both! Others around us (still trying to row the boat) begin to show the signs of stress that we feel.

A woman shared with me her story. She had invited her friend, a single mother with four children, to live with her and her husband until her affairs were straightened out, an indefinite period. "I did not pray about this decision," she told me, "and I really pushed my husband into agreement, telling him that it was obviously God's will. Never mind that our house was very small, and I was also caring for my elderly parents, who lived nearby. Thank God, my friend decided to take a job in another city. Looking back, I can see [that taking her in] would probably have destroyed my health and my marriage."

God does not force wisdom on us if we choose not to ask but to move ahead impulsively on our own initiative.

But why does God allow us to leap out of our boats? Why did Jesus say to Peter, "Come"? Why didn't he simply tell Peter to stay where he was? God gives us free will, which means we have permission to do unwise things. God does not force wisdom on us if we choose not to ask but to move ahead impulsively on our own initiative. Peter did not ask for guidance. He told Jesus to prove himself, and this was the test that he, Peter, chose to give.

I read somewhere that if we do not say to God, "*Thy* will be done," God will say to us in sorrow, "Very well, then *thy* will be done!" and we are left with the consequences of our own destructive choices.

When Jesus said to Peter as Peter sank, "You of little faith, why did you doubt?" was he referring not to Peter's sinking but to Peter's doubt that it was Jesus' voice and presence coming across the waves?

It is significant that when Jesus caught and held Peter, he did *not* tell him to keep trying to walk on the water. Jesus brought him directly and firmly back to the boat, which Peter should never have left in the first place.

Life within God's guidance is not a life of cold caution.

But does God never call us out of our "comfort zone"? Are we never to leave the ordinary ways of life, take risks?

In the first place, the disciples' task of rowing the boat against the wind was hardly a comfort zone! Their whole life with Jesus, though full of comfort, was not comfortable. They experienced joy, turbulence, and green pastures, but they also endured "valleys of the shadow." Living within God's guidance does not mean living a life of cold caution. Our life in Christ is already full of adventure. But sometimes the adventure is rowing the boat until we reach the "other side" with all its challenges.

How hard it can be to tell the difference between God's guidance and our own impetuous enthusiasms! Here are some questions we can ask ourselves:

- *Am I neglecting a major responsibility to which I am already committed?* Many people in the serving professions, perhaps especially in the ministry, put their spouses and children last. Every committee meeting, every unexpected demand, every project comes before time, energy, and emotional involvement with their family. "God comes first" is the reason they give. But the church is *not* God. Commitment to God is to be shown in *all* the areas of our lives, including the church. The commitment of a marriage vow is just as holy as the vow of ordination.

  I was surprised and impressed thirty years ago when I heard a pastor make an unheard-of remark (in those days): "When I schedule a talk or an outing with my wife, I put it on my calendar and regard it as firm a commitment as attending a church committee meeting."

- *Do I really have the stamina and energy to undertake extra projects, no matter how worthy?* "Which of you, intending to build a tower, does not first sit down and estimate the cost, to see whether he has enough to complete it?" Jesus said with direct realism (Luke 14:28). Am I impossibly crowding my day? Is any space left for rest and renewal? Is the quality of my work diminishing? Is my physical health giving me signals? I often think of our bodies as our best spiritual directors. They tell us much truth about our choices.

- *How will my decision affect those around me?* Who will have to row the boat while I am out walking on the water? Are others around me beginning to show new signs of stress? Are they bearing the burdens of my fatigue, irritability, and unfinished work while I overextend myself?

- *Am I taking on this job because I have genuine love and gifts for this project, or only because it is a worthy task and* someone *has to do it?* As a student pastor, I learned the hard way to ask this question. I had been offered a summer ministry of surveying four hundred homes in a new development of a large western city that had no community church, and I was to organize the nucleus of a church. I did not pray about my decision. God would see me through! Within a day I realized I had made a bad mistake. What would have been genuine and exciting guidance for another type of person was all wrong for me. This was not my work. I dreaded the very prospect of it once I was on the scene and really looked at what it involved. I began to "sink." The first week, in a state of total denial, I holed up in my apartment, lying on the sofa, reading mysteries, and munching on chocolates. By the second week, I realized that I was really out on the water, committed for several months to a job for which I was totally unfit. "Lord, save me!" I inwardly cried like Peter (or in words to that effect).

There was no place to go except into God's hands. As John Milton put it, "through the dear might of Him that walked the waves"[1] I was empowered to get off the sofa, walk out of the door, get myself to that new housing development, and start ringing doorbells.

God's hands held me up in the water and brought good out of my mistake. Somehow the work got done: a new little church was born that still thrives today. I learned some very important things about myself in the process, and admitted to God and myself that though I was upheld, that work was nonstop stressful. If I had chosen it as a permanent job instead of a temporary one of a few months, I think I would eventually have become ill.

I was later guided back to my proper "boat," the form of pastoral work for which I was guided and suited. There were still problems to solve, of course, and times when the wind blew against me, but I felt an underlying peace and a sense that I was in the right place, doing what I loved.

I believe God has great tenderness for us when in our enthusiastic pride, or in our desire to test God and ourselves, we leap into places where God has not told us to go. I believe Jesus spoke with amused warmth, not with anger, to Peter. When he got Peter back into the boat (what were the other disciples thinking?), Jesus probably said to his friends, "Now let's get back to the rowing—I'm here to work with you."

"The wind ceased," says verse 32. As the disciples went about their work, perhaps they whispered to one another that their Jesus, God's son, had been near them all the time. Even while praying in the mountains he was seeing them, holding them, and guiding them with his hands.

Reflection and Meditation

> Immediately Jesus spoke to them and said, "Take heart, it is I; do not be afraid."—Matthew 14:27

Rest your body in whatever way feels best for you. Take a few deep breaths; then breathe normally.

Quietly look with God at what is happening in your life. Do you feel you are working at tasks to which God has guided you? In what ways did you feel guided to this work? How do you feel about it now? Has it been more difficult recently? Does the wind seem to blow against you right now? Does God seem close or far away?

Have you felt special comfort from God recently? How did the comfort come?

Do you feel you need to be doing more than you are? Do you feel drawn to a new project? another responsibility?

Think of some time in the past when you decided to do more than what you were already doing, or of a time when you decided to do something altogether different. Did you pray about it? What happened as a result? As you look back on it, do you feel now that your decision was God's guidance? If so, what were the signs? If not, what were the results?

Rest, breathing quietly. When you feel ready, think about these questions: What is your present "boat"? What is the "water" you might want to walk on? What will be the consequences for others around you?

Move more deeply into inner quietness. What do you feel God saying?

Try with honesty to say, "God, if it is really you, what is it you want me to do?"

When you feel ready, move quietly out of your meditation. In the days to come, stay alert for definite signs of guidance.

---

1. John Milton, "Lycidas," line 173.

chapter 6

the touch that raises and releases us

Then some people came, bringing to him a paralyzed man,
carried by four of them. And when they could not bring him
to Jesus because of the crowd, they removed the roof above
him; and after having dug through it, they let down the mat
on which the paralytic lay. When Jesus saw their faith, he said
to the paralytic, "Son, your sins are forgiven. . . . I say to you,
stand up, take your mat and go to your home."

—Mark 2:3-5,11

There are times when we want to turn to God, when we
need to pray, when we know God is offering help, but we
cannot seem to move. We cannot reach out a hand to take
God's gift. We cannot summon up the will or the energy to
do something positive for ourselves.

Perhaps this inner paralysis arises from depression. Or we may be deeply grieving. Perhaps we are too exhausted, overwhelmed by events so out of control that no choice seems right. Some people are caught and held powerless by addiction. Many give up on themselves, feeling it is too late to change. This inner spiritual, emotional paralysis may be only a temporary block, but for some it lasts for years.

As I reread this story of the healing of the paralytic, an old prayer poem, said by children for generations, came to mind. Sometimes as a child I said this prayer when I did not want to be bothered with more serious prayer at bedtime:

Four angels 'round my bed,
two at my feet, two at my head.
Matthew, Mark, Luke, and John,
bless the bed that I lie on.

Guiltily I would feel that this was a superficial, poor excuse for a prayer, but it was probably better than nothing. Now I wonder if this prayer is deeper than I realized. It gives witness to the love, both human and divine, that holds and supports us especially when we are the most vulnerable and powerless, as in sleep and at other times when we cannot help ourselves.

I wonder if the paralyzed man remembered some equivalent Hebrew prayer as his four friends lifted his mat and carried him to Jesus. We do not know if he had asked for their help. It might not have occurred to him that anything could be done for him. Or he might not have been able to speak, or he might even have been unconscious. It was *their* faith that carried him. It was their faith and determination that lifted him up the steps to the roof when they saw that crowds blocked the door to the house. It was their determination that dug through the roof, "made an opening," as some translations put it.

We can imagine Jesus' face as he watched the four men breathing heavily, sweating as they lowered the helpless man in front of him. He looked first at them, seeing the power of their faith that had carried the human burden through the streets, hauled him to the roof, scratched a hole through the plaster, and brought him to Jesus' feet.

I think of people who have nearly died, or remained unconscious for a long time, or are recovering from anesthesia, or are convalescing after a stroke, who later tell us how deeply aware they were of the strength and love of those who cared for them—the ones who held their hands, talked to them, read to them, prayed with them when they could not respond.

I think of those times when I have felt stalled, unclear, too tired to make decisions or to think or pray deeply. This has sometimes happened in the midst of writing a book. Inspiration dries up; nothing moves. The temptation is to let the project drop, or to push myself with willpower and gritted teeth and produce a dead book. I am learning at these times to contact one or two trusted friends and ask them to carry me for awhile in prayer. Or I may ask them to sit and talk with me about my confused and blocked condition, *not* to tell me what to do, but to listen prayerfully, ask clarifying questions, and share perceptions. It is a miracle how such prayer and sharing opens the roof of whatever is blocking me. It is a miracle how the healing flow is released within me.

Sometimes, though, those who care about us need to be more assertive as they carry us. Some people are caught and paralyzed in downward spirals of depression or addiction. One woman did not fully understand what was happening to her. Each day it was harder to get out of bed. Her job and family responsibilities became impossible to fulfill. Letters and unpaid bills piled up. Vaguely she knew that prayer, exercise, and stress reduction would help, but the very thought of these actions made her tired. Family members did their best to help her, shouldering more than their share of household tasks, but the situation just grew worse.

Finally the family came to her rescue. One evening they all sat down with her and told her honestly what they saw happening to her and them. With loving firmness they insisted she see a physician and a therapist. They made the appointments, and one of them went with her to the physician to take notes. Tests showed an underactive thyroid, and prescribed medication helped enormously. She also began, with a therapist's help, to explore early unhealed emotional wounds that had festered deep in her heart for many years. She began to pray, not long meditations but talking to God through the day, sharing with God how she felt. When fatigue overcame her, she learned to sit down for a few minutes; take a few slow, deep breaths; and help her body release its stiffness. She began to feel new hope and strength. Eventually she decided to change jobs and enrolled in a stress reduction course. For a long time her way of praying did not include long meditations or lengthy intercessions but talking to God at intervals through the day. As she bathed, dressed, ate her meals, drove to work, and lay down to sleep, she thought of these daily actions as symbols of God's loving care enfolding and guiding her. Sometimes she imagined herself resting on a green hillside, breathing in the greenness and the light of God.

"It was God through my family who carried me out of that dark despair," she said later. "They lovingly told me the truth; they carried me with their faith and love when I could do nothing for myself. They carried me until I could begin to move again and make choices for myself."

If we are accustomed to the serving, giving role, it is extraordinarily hard to learn to be served, carried, even for a short time. But when we do allow our friends to pick us up in our emotional or spiritual paralysis and carry us to the sources of healing, we are brought closer to our humanity—a word I like better than humility.

This story of the paralyzed man is one of the few times that Jesus connects sin to illness. In most of his healings he does not make this connection, but in this case he saw that the man needed forgiveness as well as healing. The man needed a special kind of release.

What is more, Jesus called the man "son." Seldom did he call someone son or daughter. I think that he did so on occasions when he knew the person carried a lot of inner shame (deserved or not) and needed the intimate tenderness of being a son or daughter to Jesus. Perhaps this man carried an uncleansed burden of wrongdoing and, because of his sudden illness, he had not been able to repent publicly or make restitution. As usual, Jesus saw beyond the outer bodily affliction to the inner need and touched him on those deeper levels.

What faithful persons in our own lives have been present to give us their strength when we had none? Did they come to us separately or together? Did the help come from people or another source, such as the beauty and power of nature, mountains, trees, rivers, stars, gardens? Or did God touch us through a special book, music, art, a beloved animal? God reaches us through many avenues of love when we feel powerless.

When my husband was receiving a blood transfusion in a room full of patients undergoing chemotherapy, suddenly the door opened, and in walked a woman with a huge dog that had curly, long white hair. She told us she had rescued him as an abandoned and abused puppy. He seemed to feel a special love for the sick and weak. Several times a week she brought her dog to the chemotherapy room. We watched him slowly walk from person to person. He would stand in front of each person, looking up into his or her face with loving, thoughtful eyes. Occasionally he would lay his head briefly on someone's knee. After he and his owner (a former nurse) left, we all felt as if a special angel had walked among us. A new light and warmth suffused the room.

Sometimes the Holy Spirit comes to us directly. When we face a situation that we know is too big for us, whose challenge we cannot meet with human wisdom or strength, we can pray what I call the Prayer of the Rope's End:

God, this is too big for me. Take over. *Take over all the way.*
I give myself to your strong heart. Lift me, pray for me,
enfold me.

The result of this prayer is miraculous. God's own self picks
us up, makes an opening, brings us to the Source: God brings us
to God in our great weakness. As Romans 8:26 says,

> The Spirit helps us in our weakness; for we do not know how
> to pray as we ought, but that very Spirit intercedes with sighs
> too deep for words.

Reflection and Meditation

> I say to you, stand up, take your mat and go to your home.
>
> —Mark 2:11

Rest your body, your whole self, on the underlying strength of
God. Breathe slowly and fully, then naturally. Every breath is
God's Spirit breathing into you.

When you feel ready, recall a time when you were so tired,
depressed, or confused that you could not make choices or do
anything to help yourself. Think of a time when even prayer
seemed too much of an effort, a time when your inner strength
was gone. Perhaps you remember a time when you felt powerless
in just one aspect of your life. What happened? Did someone
reach out to you? Did someone or something give you strength
until you could move again, reach out, stand on your feet, and
make choices?

As you reflect on that time, do you feel God was reaching out and touching you through those helpers? Did help come in some other way? Did God's Spirit come directly and carry you?

Rest quietly, and give grateful thanks for the help that came, in whatever way it came. Look with God at this experience and reflect on its meaning.

Do you feel a sense of powerlessness in any part of your life right now? Is there some area in your life in which you cannot seem to move, change, or make choices even if you want to? Tell God how you feel. Say with honesty to God that you feel powerless over part of your life. Tell God if you feel that your whole life has become stalled, inert.

Ask God to take over that part of your life, to take over your whole life and carry you with the power of the Holy Spirit, to pray in you and for you. Ask God to send you others who will share their strength with you for a while until your strength returns. Rest in God, knowing that help and empowerment are already enfolding you.

Look at the days to come. Do you face a situation that seems too much for you, too overwhelming? A doctor's appointment? a new responsibility? a family problem? something else?

Ask the risen Jesus to go ahead of you and prepare the way, the time, the place. Think of the Christ in that future place, filling it with light and strength, so that when you get there, you will feel peace and empowerment.

Rest quietly, gently breathing God's breath. Know that God already holds that future experience in God's healing hands and heart. When you feel ready, slowly and quietly return from your meditation.

chapter 7

the eyes that find and free us

Now he was teaching in one of the synagogues on the sabbath. And just then there appeared a woman with a spirit that had crippled her for eighteen years. She was bent over and was quite unable to stand up straight. When Jesus saw her, he called her over and said, "Woman, you are set free from your ailment." When he laid his hands on her, immediately she stood up straight and began praising God.

—Luke 13:10-13

Sometimes the transforming Presence heals us, changes us when we are expecting nothing, asking for nothing. We are living our usual constricted life, taking it for granted, and then suddenly everything changes.

A scientist, whom I have known well for many years, stood in a large crowd at a healing service. He noticed a woman standing in front of him, her withered leg held by a brace. As far as he could tell, she was not expecting anything special. She had not gone to the front of the room for a healing touch, nor did she have any friend with her who offered to take her forward. Apparently she was just standing there, looking on.

He noticed she began to rub her leg rather restlessly but did not look down. As he watched, her shrunken leg began to lengthen and fill out right before his eyes. Obviously she felt her leg brace become desperately uncomfortable and constricting. Then she looked down.

Luke's story of the bent-over woman implies that she also was expecting nothing. She had been crippled for eighteen years and probably took her condition for granted by now. This was just the way things were, her everyday reality. She had not asked Jesus for healing, and, unlike the paralyzed man, apparently had no faithful friend who believed Jesus could help her. The whole community took her condition for granted. There was no taint of shame or contamination as with the bleeding woman; she was just part of the village's everyday reality.

The story says the woman appeared. Had she been standing in the women's section of the synagogue, and Jesus suddenly noticed her? Had she hobbled in late? Or was she perhaps walking slowly past the open door? Whatever the case, his compassionate eyes found her, and he called her to come to him. Undoubtedly this shocked everyone. The setting was not, after all, a private home or a street corner. It was in a synagogue on the sabbath. Jesus was up front preaching from the scriptures during a solemn hour that was sacred to God. But then suddenly he interrupted himself to call a woman to come through the crowd of men to the front of the synagogue. He was breaking every tradition in an appallingly public way.

The woman hobbled forward, probably trying to avoid the outraged eyes around her. Why had he called her? Had she done something wrong? What was going to happen?

Jesus touched her and spoke with gentle authority: "Lady,[1] you are set free from your ailment." Did she feel a sudden onrush of new strength? Or did she notice a sudden change in her body, an impossible change? It was Jesus who touched her, but it was *she* who "straightened herself up" (Luke 13:13, GNT).

For the first time in years she could take a deep breath from uncramped lungs. For the first time she could lift her arms high, throw back her head in the ancient posture of praise, and cry out in thanksgiving to God.

From what scripture had Jesus been teaching when she appeared? We are not told, but I like to think it was from his beloved book of Isaiah, perhaps from the prophetic, ecstatic chapter 35:

> Then the eyes of the blind shall be opened,
>   and the ears of the deaf unstopped;
> then the lame shall leap like a deer,
>   and the tongue of the speechless sing for joy.
> For waters shall break forth in the wilderness,
>   and streams in the desert;
> the burning sand shall become a pool,
>   and the thirsty ground springs of water.
>
> —Isaiah 35:5-7

This radiant vision, this compassionate power, reveals the God who longs to set us free, to release us, to make us whole. This passage describes Jesus' whole life, each of his acts of wonder.

God's passion flashes forth in Jesus' anger when the legalistic synagogue leader rails against Jesus for healing on the sabbath, the day of rest. One can almost hear the quiet fierceness in Jesus' reply: "'You hypocrites! Does not each of you on the sabbath untie his ox . . . and lead it away to give it water? And ought not this woman, a daughter of Abraham whom Satan bound *for eighteen long years,* be set free from this bondage on the sabbath day?" (Luke 13:15-16, italics mine).

This is the anger of God's own self when we block the full streams of God's compassion and healing with legalistic tradition. As with his other miracles, Jesus longed to set free not only the individual but also the communal body from its spiritual bondage to a new, released life within God.

As with so many other of his acts of healing, Jesus not only set free this woman's body but also her spirit. The years of a cramped, constricted body may well have cramped and constricted her feelings about herself. Her community did not look on her as shameful or as a sinner, but undoubtedly they thought of her as inferior. Jesus publicly called her a "daughter of Abraham," the only time that particular designation of rich and honorable dignity is used in scripture. He knew she needed this title of dignity and worth. She moved forward now into her new life, not only standing tall bodily but also spiritually. She had been set free in every way.

Does the unexpected releasing touch of God come to us today? Has a door in our inner prisons of the spirit, which we have sadly believed to be our only reality, suddenly, unexpectedly been opened?

Many people have shared with me their unexpected awareness that their church, their spiritual community and its set of beliefs, has become for them an emotional, spiritual prison. For many years they accepted the rigid will of their community as the will of God, submitting to an inflexible, narrow outlook.

Then a deep restlessness, a new longing, began within these persons. Rebellious thoughts arose that at first they tried to quench as demonic temptations. Health began to deteriorate; dreams became escape dreams. They wondered if their new restlessness and bodily signals were a wake-up call from God. They paid attention to the growing sense of pressure and discomfort the way the crippled woman my friend observed paid attention to the confining leg brace and finally looked at her new, expanding life.

This sudden change can happen in an unhappy, increasingly constricted job situation. One of my cousins, successful in his line of work for many years, began to feel the pinch of his spirit. He paid attention to his deepest longings and became a gifted wood carver and stained-glass artist.

The touch can come to us in a family situation in which we have, only half-consciously, felt trapped for years. We may with surprise realize that we have been the sole burden bearer of the family, the leaning post for everyone. We may have been thrust into the position of peacemaker or problem solver, and we may have accepted that role, not admitting to ourselves how stifling, how cramped is that role.

I have seen the wake-up call in marriages that have lost their love, hope, vitality. The husband or wife may have been living for years in a hopeless, resigned condition. Then something happens, a crisis of some sort. Perhaps one of them falls in love with someone else. Does this necessarily mean either an affair or the end of the marriage? It may instead be a symptom of long-term unhappiness that God wants the couple to look at: a chronic emotional hopelessness or woundedness that may have deep roots in the past, whose time for healing has come.

The Spirit always calls us to rebirth, new life.

❦

Whatever the outcome, I do not believe the God who inspired that thirty-fifth chapter of Isaiah in which the tongues of the speechless will sing for joy, and in which waters will spring forth from the desert, ever wants us to live a life of deep, stifled unhappiness. The Spirit always calls us to rebirth, new life.

Sometimes God's new life requires us to look with honesty at abuse that may be poisoning our commitments, whether in our families, our churches, or our workplaces. Some abuses go back for generations, causing deep dysfunction in our families. Sometimes abuses have crept only recently into our situation. Some can be healed through honest sharing, love, and prayer. Sometimes they cannot be healed in this life. If a relationship or commitment is destroying the light within us—if our hope, health, and vitality are deteriorating—it is better to release ourselves from that relationship than to let ourselves be spiritually and emotionally destroyed. We may need to act as Jesus did when he left his hometown, Nazareth, and even his mother and brothers for a while when they tried to destroy or suppress his ministry (Luke 4:28-30 and Mark 3:21).

There are so many ways of being trapped, constricted, bent over. It is not God's will, as we see through Jesus, that we remain in that condition.

Jesus was keenly aware of the world's hunger and pain. He had far more to say about that than he did about sin. Somehow through the centuries we have forgotten this truth. Many church liturgies and much spiritual teaching still emphasize sin but say little about the burden of unhealed suffering; the prisons of unrelenting grief, shame, fear; the generations of wounded families projecting their burdens on the next generations; the hurt, anger, and fear among races and nations.

How can we help one another to see the pain as Jesus saw the bent-over woman? How can we learn to name what we see and to bring the crushing burdens to God's heart and hands?

How do we begin with *our* own pain and inner prisons? If we, as wounded healers, are not aware of our own wounds, our own constricting burdens—if we are not being healed and released, we will invariably inflict more suffering on those we wish to help; we will pull others into our inner prisons.

How can we best respond when God's eyes find us, fasten on our burden, and God calls us to come closer?

Reflection and Meditation

> She was bent over and was quite unable to stand up straight. When Jesus saw her, he called her over and said, "Woman, you are set free from your ailment."—Luke 13:11-12

Let your whole body quietly rest in God's presence. Slowly and deeply breathe; then breathe naturally.

When you feel ready, ask God to show you if there is a constriction in your life. Do you feel bent over, cramped, held in, held down in any way? Do you feel unfree, trapped?

Look quietly with God at this inner prison, this heavy burden. Put into words what you feel. Name it to God.

Where do you feel your burden comes from? A relationship? a commitment? the work you are doing? your family? a childhood of repression and dysfunction? Maybe you cannot tell why you feel it.

Reflect on Jesus' words at the beginning of his ministry:

> "The Spirit of the Lord is upon me,
>   because he has anointed me . . .
> to proclaim release to the captives . . .
>   to let the oppressed go free."—Luke 4:18

The Christ who sets us free is with you now. Have you felt any recent change? a restlessness? a new longing? a change in dreams? other changes? Look at these feelings with God in this safe place. Is God speaking to you through these changes?

God wants to free you, to release you into new life, to open the prison door, to take your heaviness off you.

God calls you closer. If you feel ready, give to God's heart your inner burden or constriction—whatever you feel traps you and enslaves you.

Know that there will be changes. They may be outer changes in your way of life or your relationships. Or there may be an inner transformation that sets you free. You will straighten yourself up. You will move with empowered freedom again. You will be able to lift your whole self in God's praise.

When you feel ready, take a few deep breaths; lightly massage your face and hands; stretch; and quietly leave your meditation.

---

1. I found this form of address in the *Jewish New Testament*, translated from the original Greek by David H. Stern (Jerusalem: Jewish New Testament Publications, 1989).

chapter 8

the presence that transforms us

> When it was evening on that day, the first day of the week, and the doors of the house where the disciples had met were locked for fear. . . . , Jesus came and stood among them and said, "Peace be with you." After he said this, he showed them his hands and his side. Then the disciples rejoiced when they saw the Lord. Jesus said to them again, "Peace be with you. As the Father has sent me, so I send you." When he had said this, he breathed on them and said to them, "Receive the Holy Spirit."
>
> —John 20:19-22

Transformation is the greatest miracle of all! More wondrous than the healing of the body is the re-creation of the whole person into newness of life: "So if anyone is in Christ, there is a new creation: everything old has passed away; see, everything has become new!" (2 Cor. 5:17).

I used to wonder why Jesus' first miracle was changing water into wine at the wedding feast in Cana. It seemed an undignified way to begin his ministry. Why wasn't his first act of wonder something more lofty, like a healing? Later I understood. God came into the world through Jesus to fill us with new, divine life, which is the true meaning of being "born again."

The infusion of a new life—a new way of relating to God, self, and others—underlies all Jesus' miracles. As we study his acts of wonder, we see that along with bodily healing came the healing of deeper wounds of shame, exclusion, sin, fear, hopelessness. New joy, faith, love, commitment flooded into those whose bodies he had healed, whose shame and fear had been calmed.

"We were water. He changed us into wine!" was a popular saying in the early church. Or as a spiritual teacher once said, "Jesus meets us where we are, but he doesn't leave us there."

The disciples, hiding in that locked room after Jesus' crucifixion, felt and acted like hunted victims. Their beloved leader was gone, destroyed by the combined powers of religion and politics. They were the next in line. What could they possibly do? Even if Jesus *had* come back to life, as some had rumored, he would not trust them again, the ones who had deserted him in Gethsemane. All that they had lived for, had loved and served for years, was gone.

But within days they came out of their locked rooms into the streets, boldly witnessing about Jesus and his kingdom. Certainly the force of shame and willpower did not release and send them forth. Something radical had happened. Their transformation lasted through their lifetime; no one ever turned back. The power of terrorized victimhood changed into the power of joyful devotion.

In an earlier book I described an experience in my early teens that opened doors and began a great change within me. My beloved grandmother had a heart attack in the middle of the night. I was awakened by lights and the sounds of running feet, telephone calls, and her low cries of pain. As the doctor arrived and ran up the stairs, I turned my back on the whole terrifying scene, went into my bedroom, closed the door, went into my closet, shutting that door also, and then sat on the floor in the dark. I did not weep or pray. I just sat there, icy cold in shock. There was nothing to be done. My grandmother, a close friend and companion all my life, was leaving, leaving in pain. I sat there, staring into the dark.

Then someone came through the door and stood in front of me, someone I could neither see nor hear. The closet door was still closed, but someone had come in anyhow and was there with me. I felt strong, warm hands grasping mine. It was not exactly a physical touch; it was more like hands beneath bodily hands. I was pulled to my feet. Warmth flowed into my body. A sense of total comfort and strength enfolded me. I opened the door and went out.

My grandmother died peacefully the next day. I knew she was safe and that all was well with her, and also with me. Something deep had changed in me. I had been a timid, nervous child. Now a new opening occurred within me: a deeper trust in God, myself, and others.

I began to study the scriptures for the first time. Though the terrors of World War II surrounded us, I realized that if God was really like Jesus, as the Bible said, then the universe and all of us in this scary world were held in hands of love, and ultimately we were safe.

The change in me took several years, but the *central* transformation was given that night when someone came through the closed doors and enfolded my hands and heart.

For the disciples too, as they huddled in the locked room, the Presence came through the closed door and gave them shalom, or vibrant peace. God does not kick down doors or come in to scold, shame, and condemn. Any religion or spirituality that does such things is not of the Holy Spirit. Not one word of condemnation did Jesus say. He spoke words of comfort and peace. He showed the disciples his wounds so they would know he was neither a ghost nor an impostor, to let them know he still shared their humanness and always would.

Then Jesus gave them an incredible gift. Before they unlocked the doors, set foot into the streets, demonstrated one act of courage, or spoke Jesus' name openly in the city, he breathed on them the gift and power of the Holy Spirit and then gave them a mission of trust. He loved his friends, believed in them, and endowed them while they were still locked in that room.

What indescribable comfort comes to us through this story. God is with us behind our defensive walls, our locked doors. The doors are not kicked in, nor are the walls and masks torn away. God understands that our walls and masks grew from our pain and fear, from traumas that affected our ability to trust. In time the doors themselves will be healed, and our masks will become living flesh again when we realize we no longer need them for our survival. But in the meantime, the healing love shines in our defended darkness, and God's Holy Spirit is breathed upon us.

God understands that our walls and masks grew from our pain and fear, from traumas that affected our ability to trust.

John's Gospel tells us that a week later as the disciples gathered, the door was locked *again*. One would think that, having seen the risen Jesus and breathed in his loving power, the disciples (and we) would never need to lock a door again. But we do, of course. Our hearts may be bonded to Christ, and we may be transformed at our center, but old responses, old habits of fear, take longer to give way. Again Jesus stood among them inside their locked room, and with infinite tenderness he led Thomas through his doubts into trust. There was no angry reproach, but gentle, persistent healing. God has renounced force over us. Power is not the same as force. The transformation begins at our center and works its way outward with gentle power, the way green shrubs work upward from deep within the soil, the way yeast expands within the loaf, transforming it into bread.

Sometimes we feel that though we have given ourselves wholly to God, we have walled off *parts* of ourselves—inner corners and closets of old hurt, anger, fear, shame. We don't want anyone, even God, to look at or handle those areas. We closed the doors on them because they are so sensitive, and we fear being hurt again. They are like sealed-off infections dating from early childhood or adolescence. Most of the time we try to ignore these pockets of inner, shadowed pain, but often they break through in ways that appall us—through phobias or sudden inappropriate rage, panic, or irrationality.

"Mostly I act and feel like a grown-up, mature person," one woman told me. "But when I feel left out of things, unwanted, excluded, unneeded, I feel inwardly like an angry child bursting into tears. I brood, lash out at others, become critical, or act like a martyr. Deep down, I have such an icy fear of being left alone. But I'm a bit scared of trying to find out where it comes from. I don't want to look at it."

When we know we have locked off areas of pain that are not ready for change or healing, Christ's love does not assault us. It is enough for a while to think of loving light quietly shining on our defended areas. It is enough for a while to think of the Christ gently touching the fear and pain hiding there, reaching into our depths for the crying ones who are buried so deep we do not consciously hear their cries. We do not have to go there and look at them ourselves until we feel ready.

Deep gifts are also being touched and released in those hidden places. The pain is being transformed into new, undreamed-of powers within us. It is enough for a while just to give consent to the deep, transforming healing that is taking place.

In time, the locks will melt, the doors will be healed, and we will be able to look at the pain we have hidden for so long. We do not have to look by ourselves. The risen Christ looks and understands with us. In time, new power and beauty will come forth from those shadows.

The day after my husband died, something strange and beautiful happened at my house. Only recently did I connect this incident, the Easter night story, with my experience in the closet while my grandmother was dying.

We were all tired, busy, and struggling with loss and grief. The phone was ringing; people were coming and going; flowers were arriving; and arrangements were being made for the newspaper announcements and the memorial service. That evening in the midst of the clamor we all heard the sound of soft singing in the house.

Where was it coming from? No radio was playing. The television wasn't on. The windows were closed. After some bewildered looking around, we traced the singing to the hall coat closet. Opening the door, we saw three of my young grandchildren sitting crowded together in the small, dark place. They weren't crying, nor did they look frightened. They looked peaceful as they sang. "The music is *beautiful*," we said. "But *why* are you crammed into a closet, and why are you singing?"

They couldn't explain exactly why. "We just felt like singing in the closet." Now I know why. God was revealing to me once again that there is always love, comfort, and singing—even in our darkest closets.

Reflection and Meditation

> Jesus came and stood among them and said, "Peace be with you." . . . he breathed on them and said to them, "Receive the Holy Spirit."—John 20:19, 22

The Christ stands among us in risen power. Relax your body, your heart in that presence. Breathe slowly and deeply the breath of the new life. Then just breathe naturally.

With the knowledge that God's tenderness enfolds you, ask yourself if something within you is afraid, even of God. Does some part of you want to hide behind closed doors, away from intimacy, away from new ways of being healed, new ways of living? Is there something in you that does not want to be looked at?

Picture or just think of that part of you hiding like Jesus' disciples in the locked room, seeking protection from something that is hard to face. Does this wish to hide stem from some shock, fear, betrayal of trust, abuse, fear of rejection? an incident long ago or recent?

Think of or picture that locked place as filled with gentle light, with a presence that does not force open the door but still is with you, bringing comfort. This presence may feel like someone you know and utterly trust.

Warmth fills you. The fear and reluctance begin slowly to move away. The door is still locked. You are free to choose. But the door itself is being healed. You are not rebuked or shamed. Trust often grows slowly.

A gift is already being given you—God's own Spirit. God believes in you and says: "When you are ready to come forth, I have special work for you, special places for you to go. And I will be with you at every step."

Rest and breathe quietly, letting the light and the empowered gift begin to grow in your inner room, in your heart.

If you feel ready, let that inner, hidden part of you open the door and come forth. If you are not yet ready for this step, know that the healing light will continue to shine in quiet power in your room until the lock itself is healed. When the time is right, you will move forth in hope and joy.

Rest quietly, giving thanks that God's healing and transforming light already shines deep within you.

When you are ready, notice your steady, quiet breathing. Lightly massage your face and hands, and gently leave your meditation.

chapter 9

"but there are also many other things"

But there are also many other things that Jesus did; if every one of them were written down, I suppose that the world itself could not contain the books that would be written.

—John 21:25

The four Gospels conclude with such mysterious words. What were these "many other things that Jesus did"? We long to know. Why didn't someone at least begin to write all those books that the world could not contain? I have sometimes thought that *we* are those books!

The book of Acts follows John's Gospel. Each one of us who loves Jesus is a book of Acts through which the risen Jesus shows the eyes of God that find us, the voice of God that reaches us, the hands of God that hold us, and the heart of God that heals the hungry, weeping world.

What manner of book will we each become? What life will unfold and take form when we are healed and transformed? This book has looked at seven of Jesus' acts of wonder and the different ways the hurts and needs were shown to him: the one who called out boldly in faith, those who screamed in panic, the one who reached out in silence and shame, the one who could not move a finger to help himself, the one who sank when going faster than guidance, the one who had asked for and expected nothing, and those who hid as victims behind locked doors. So many ways of asking! And in each case Jesus saw the deepest need and touched the deepest hurt—in whatever way that person most needed it.

But what happened next? What became of each person after the healing touch, the profound transformation? My husband and I had hoped to write a book titled *And The Next Day* in which we would reflect on the life of each person Jesus touched.

How did the formerly bleeding woman and the bent-over woman live out the rest of their lives in villages that had grown accustomed to their disabilities? What might have become of Bartimaeus as he followed Jesus to Jerusalem? What happened to the paralyzed man when he walked again with strength? Did he stay in his community or leave? Did he keep in touch with his four faithful friends?

Scripture does not tell us. We do know that some of those whom Jesus healed and befriended left home and followed him on the road, at least for a while. Some he told, "Go home to your friends, and tell them how much the Lord has done for you, and what mercy he has shown you" (Mark 5:19).

Mary, Martha, and their brother, Lazarus, whom Jesus called from death, apparently kept their home as a center of welcome and refreshment for Jesus and those others who walked with him on the road.

The disciples' mission was to spread the good news of Jesus' resurrection and God's all-embracing love. Most of them traveled far. Some stayed in Jerusalem.

What about us? What will be our mission? What sort of persons will we be as the love of God increasingly fills us and shines through us? One of John's letters says mysteriously and provocatively:

> Beloved, we are God's children now;
> what we will be has not yet been revealed.
> What we do know is this: when [Christ] is revealed,
> we will be like him, for we will see him as he is.
>
> —1 John 3:2

As Christ increasingly reveals himself in us, we will increasingly become who we are meant to be. What that will be is not shown in advance. Our own special mission will unfold in a way that seems so natural, and yet as we look back on it, so surprising.

We know this: we will not resemble one another. As said earlier, when God transforms us, we become even more uniquely ourselves, more distinct. As Christ's face increasingly reveals itself in our faces, our identity is not obliterated, but a brighter light shines through us. God does not melt us down. We stand forth, for each one of us becomes a miracle unlike all others.

Jesus himself was miracle. More than what he did or said was what he was and is. That living presence still shows us supremely the heart and face of God. That gentle, loving touch still reaches through time and space to touch our deepest need.

Because Jesus is miracle, we too become miracles, living in God's realm that Jesus called the kingdom.

Because Jesus is miracle, we too become miracles, living in God's realm that Jesus called the kingdom. We do not have to die to enter God's kingdom; it is already at work on earth—unfolding, expanding, healing, bringing new life. God's kingdom is the realm in which daily miracles on all levels are a natural occurrence.

Perhaps words like *kingdom* or *realm* do not feel quite real to us. Even the word *heaven* brings up images that feel remote and irrelevant to our daily lives. How can we name the living, enfolding power of God's love that surrounds us?

The scriptures use powerful symbols to describe God's presence: light, wind, breath, rivers, fountains, mountains, wings, hands, arms, feasts, fruitful shrubs and vines, mother and father, lover, marriage. I love most to speak of the heart of God.

This heart, this realm, calls us into *relationship*, not a code of laws or a theological creed. We are to be bonded in love, not in bondage to a taskmaster. Out of this relationship of beloved to beloved grows the miracle we are and will be. Jesus made this so clear as he talked to his disciples the night before his death:

> Abide in me as I abide in you. Just as the branch cannot bear fruit by itself unless it abides in the vine, neither can you unless you abide in me. I am the vine, you are the branches.
> —John 15:4-5

He speaks here of a *connectedness*, a deep receiving of God's life, from which all transformation comes, from which our new life will rise.

Some of us will be called to other places and new relationships. Some of us will be asked to stay where we are and show what God has done for us. If we give what we are to God and enter that divine relationship, no vocation is by definition holier than another. We do not need to become ministers or missionaries unless that is our specific guidance. One of the holiest men I ever knew was a microbiologist. One of the holiest women I ever knew was a librarian. If we belong to God, whatever our vocation, God will shine through us.

If we belong to God, whatever our vocation, God will shine through us.

Increasingly I find that for me, the most direct way to healing, transformation, and guidance is to give explicitly to God's heart each bodily pain, each wave of anger or fear, each embarrassment, each perplexity, each inner confusion, each person for whom I pray.

I know God's heart will take what is offered, hold it, heal it, and transform it into the creative energy it is meant to be.

I am learning to release past hurtful memories, as well as challenging future events, to God's heart. I am learning to send to that heart my experiences right now: driving, cleaning, phoning, writing, taking a walk, entering a plane, welcoming my family at the door.

Not only can we release our needs, hurts, and perplexities to God's heart but also the little daily joys, comforts, beauties, laughter, and work well done. We can share feelings of thankfulness and praise, even for the smallest things, with God's heart throughout the day.

I think of the bent-over woman each time she got out of bed and stood tall, each time she reached up to a high shelf. I think of the bleeding, ostracized woman each time she put her arms around a friend. I think of the paralyzed man each time he stretched his legs and walked out the door.

I think of my own healing from paralyzing shyness each time I speak in front of a group. I think of my friend who wakes each day with eagerness rather than in depression. All these living hearts are bonded with God's living heart.

No wonder John said that if everything were written down, the world could not contain all the books about God's loving acts of wonder. Years ago I found a hymn that I had never heard of, called "The Love of God." According to the author, the third stanza was found written on the walls of a mental institution by a patient. The words were not discovered until after the patient's death. God's comfort had entered his room and enfolded him:

> Could we with ink the ocean fill,
> And were the skies of parchment made,
> Were every stalk on earth a quill,
> And every man a scribe by trade;
> To write the love of God above
> Would drain the ocean dry;
> Nor could the scroll contain the whole,
> Though stretched from sky to sky.[1]

Wherever the heart, hands, eyes, and voice of God call us to go, that Presence of empowered love not only holds us close but also has gone ahead of us to heal, prepare, and bless the place, the experience to come.

And when God leads us there, God's own self will be there
at the door
to welcome us and abide with us,
in a life called *miracle*.

---

1. Frederick M. Lehman, "The Love of God," 1917. Accessed at http://www.cyberhymnal.org/htm/l/o/loveofgo.htm.

about the author

F LORA SLOSSON WUELLNER has a specialized ministry of spiritual renewal and inner healing, both individual and communal. She is a teacher, retreat leader, spiritual director, and author.

Wuellner is an ordained minister in the United Church of Christ and formerly adjunct faculty at the Pacific School of Religion in Berkeley, California. She received her Master of Divinity degree from Chicago Theological Seminary and served pastorates in Wyoming, Idaho, and Illinois.

Wuellner's books include the following:
- *Enter by the Gate: Jesus' 7 Guidelines When Making Hard Choices*
- *Forgiveness, the Passionate Journey: Nine Steps of Forgiving Through Jesus' Beatitudes*
- *Prayer and Our Bodies*
- *Prayer, Stress, and Our Inner Wounds*
- *Feed My Shepherds: Spiritual Healing and Renewal for Those in Christian Leadership*

For more information about these titles,
visit www.upperroom.org/bookstore,
or call 1-800-972-0433.